High

THE COBBLER, THE PRINCESS, AND THE NEWBORN KING

WRITTEN AND ILLUSTRATED BY DAN FOOTE

Chariot Victor Publishing
A Division of Cook Communications

Chariot Victor Publishing
A Division of Cook Communications, Colorado Springs, CO 80918
Cook Communications, Paris, Ontario
Kingsway Communications, Eastbourne, England

THE COBBLER, THE PRINCESS, AND THE NEWBORN KING
© 1999 by Dan Foote

Designed by Peter Schmidt of Granite Design
First printing, 1999
Printed in Singapore
03 02 01 00 99   5 4 3 2 1

Foote, Dan.
        The cobbler, the princess, and the newborn King / written and
illustrated by Dan Foote.
                p.   cm.
        Summary: Everything changes for Rebecca, an innkeeper's daughter,
when their barn becomes the home of the newborn King.
        ISBN 0-7814-3079-8
        1.   Jesus Christ--Nativity Juvenile fiction. [1. Jesus Christ--Nativity
Fiction.] I. Title.
PZ7.F7435Co 1999
[E]--dc21
                                                        99-15576
                                                        CIP

To Amy, Ben, and Katie,

and everyone who treasures God's

perfect gift in the manger...

and for all those still to know Him.

—DAN FOOTE

Rebecca really didn't mind giving up her room. It was all part of living at the Dove's Nest Inn. She liked the kitchen anyway. Rebecca could play anything she wanted in the kitchen, and she usually wanted to play *Princess of the Castle*. Normally, her father grew tired of Rebecca's pretending, but this week he was too busy to notice. The Dove's Nest was full of all sorts of strange people from distant lands. It was so full that Princess Rebecca had to sleep in her castle.

Rebecca's father begged her, "Pleeeease stay out of trouble and don't pester the guests."

So, the princess kept a close eye on her loyal subjects from the castle tower. She saw a rich man with his harem. She saw an armored foot soldier and his shield bearer. She saw some traveling musicians and a holy man. But the one who interested Rebecca the most was the little old cobbler in the corner with the leather pouch. *Anyone who talks to himself can't be all that bad,* she thought.

Princess Rebecca secretly lowered herself from her tower and sneaked past her father. Like a cat, she ducked under the soldier's table and popped up behind the musician's lute. Rebecca crawled closer and closer until she could hear the cobbler's whispers.

She heard him mutter, "Time to get ready. The King is coming." Then, he turned and looked right at Rebecca. He smiled and asked, "Can you help?"

There was something in the twinkle of the cobbler's dark eyes. It reminded Rebecca of the north star on clear moonless nights. It made her stare. It made her feel warm inside. It made her forget all about being a princess.

The old cobbler grabbed the leather pouch in his gnarled hand and limped out the front door. He waved for Rebecca to join him. She couldn't help but follow.

The cobbler made his way through the crowded streets and to the back of the Dove's Nest. Rebecca watched cautiously from a few steps behind. The old man hobbled down the alley to the barn behind the inn.

He pointed and said, "His royal palace awaits!"

Rebecca was really starting to like the old cobbler. *He pretends almost as good as I do,* she thought.

"Come, Princess Rebecca," the cobbler called. "We must prepare for the King."

Rebecca and the old man played *The King Is Coming* all day long. They pretended the barn was the King's palace and the feeding trough was His throne. They nailed boards and repaired holes in the palace roof. They cleaned and swept and put new hay in the throne. Rebecca asked the old cobbler if he was Chief of the Palace Guards. The cobbler said he was "only a servant." Rebecca thought that showed signs of a poor imagination.

As the sun sank below the Dove's Nest, a cool breeze blew through the palace. The old man straightened up and announced, "It is time!"

The old man raced up the alley to the front of the Dove's Nest. Rebecca could hardly keep up with him. Suddenly, the cobbler stopped and bowed his head. A man leading a donkey passed by. Sitting on the donkey was a beautiful woman who was very pregnant. She smiled at Rebecca as the donkey clip-clopped to the barn.

"I'm very sorry," Rebecca heard her father say. "It's all the room I have left."

The cobbler waited until the man and the pregnant woman were gone. Then he giggled to Rebecca, "The King is almost here!"

The old cobbler ran upstairs to room 7. He burst inside, went to the window, and looked down on the barn. Rebecca joined him. They watched the man lift the pregnant woman off the donkey and place her on the new hay.

Suddenly, light filled the room. The light was coming from an oil lamp the cobbler had pulled from his leather pouch.

He said, "Princess, take this to the palace. The King will be a shining light to a dark place."

Rebecca bowed like royalty and took the lamp. It was very quiet as she walked to the barn. As Rebecca got closer, she could see the man holding the pregnant woman. The woman looked like she was in pain.

Rebecca started to feel scared. "I don't think I want to play *The King Is Coming* anymore," she said to herself.

"Could I borrow your lamp?"

Rebecca jumped.

It was the voice of the man. "My wife is about to have a baby, and I can't see a thing." Rebecca handed the man her lamp. His wife smiled and thanked her. Rebecca wasn't frightened anymore. It was very peaceful in the barn. The couple's donkey stood quietly eating hay in the back corner while a dove cooed from the loft. The neighbor's cat, Goliath, purred and rubbed his back against the gatepost.

The woman winced in pain.

"Does it hurt?" Rebecca asked.

"A little," the woman responded.

"It makes me thirsty, too."

Rebecca looked up and saw the old cobbler waving from his window. "I'll be right back," she said.

Rebecca ran up the stairs and threw open the door. The cobbler was pulling a water jug from his pouch. He handed the jug to Rebecca and said quietly, "The King comes giving living water."

Rebecca could hardly control her excitement. "She's having a baby!" she blurted out, "That lady's going to have a baby in my barn!"

The old cobbler bent down close to Rebecca and said, "Didn't I tell you the King was coming?"

Rebecca took the jug of water and asked, "Can't you give them your room?!"

The cobbler smiled sadly and said, "No. This King must suffer so that He can help others who suffer."

Rebecca tried to hand the water jug to the man, but he was too busy helping his wife. The woman held her husband tightly. She looked tired and was all out of breath. Rebecca had never seen a woman have a baby before. She wished she could remember when she was born, so she would know what happened next.

"Do you have any extra blankets?" the man asked. "I don't have anything to wrap the baby in when it comes."

Rebecca said, "My friend will."

The old cobbler was waiting at the door as Rebecca climbed the stairs. He was holding several pieces of cloth in his hands. Rebecca could see the cobbler's empty leather pouch laying on the bedroom floor. There were tears in his eyes.

He handed her the cloths and said, "Here. Take these. The King will be robed in majesty."

Rebecca looked deep into the cobbler's eyes. They sparkled brighter than ever before.

"Hurry," he whispered. "The King is here."

Rebecca first heard the noise as she ran toward the barn. It grew louder as she got closer. Someone was crying. That someone was a baby! The light from the lamp cast a glow over the whole barn. The man was holding his wife and she was holding the baby, a little red-faced crying baby. Rebecca thought they looked so happy, except for the baby, of course.

"I think He's cold," Rebecca said, handing the cloths to the father.

"It's a boy," he said.

"I know," Rebecca told him. "He's a King."

The mother and father wrapped the baby in the cloths and laid Him in the feeding trough. The baby quieted down. Rebecca stood at the gate with Goliath the cat and stared at the newborn King in His throne.

Rebecca couldn't wait to tell the cobbler about the baby. As she soared up the stairs, a bright light flashed from underneath the door. It was the brightest light Rebecca had ever seen. She covered her eyes and pushed open the door. The light was moving up and out of the window. On the floor were the cobbler's empty pouch and robe. Rebecca ran to the window.

From out of the bright light, she heard the old man's voice say, "The King has come, Princess Rebecca! The King has come!"

Rebecca stared at the light until it stopped, resting high above the barn. The light looked so familiar. It looked just like the twinkle in the old cobbler's dark eyes.

It was quiet now at the Dove's Nest and throughout all of Bethlehem. Rebecca curled up on the floor in the cobbler's robe and stared out the window. She gazed at the star over the barn. She knew she would always remember this day, the day she played *The King Is Coming*. She would always remember the young couple in her barn, the old cobbler with starlight in his eyes, and the newborn King. As Rebecca drifted off to sleep she heard angel voices echoing in the hills, "Glory to God in the highest. Peace on earth. Goodwill toward men!"

FAITH PARENTING GUIDE

The Cobbler, the Princess, and the Newborn King

Age: 4-7
Life Issue: My child enjoys hearing the story of Jesus' birth.
Value: Christmas/Faith

LEARNING STYLES

Visual Learning Style: Take note of all the sights and sounds of the Christmas season. Look for nativity scenes that decorate people's yards or store windows. Turn these into teaching moments to review the biblical account of the Savior's birth. When at home, look up the story in Luke 2:1-20 and Matthew 2:1-12 in your Bible. Read the story together.

Auditory Style: Explain the difference between a pretend story and an actual story. Read Luke 2:1-20 and Matthew 2:1-12 from a children's version of the Bible. How are these stories different? Even though the innkeeper could have had a daughter like Rebecca, we don't know for sure. The Bible has the complete true story of the Savior's birth.

Tactile Learning Style: Pretending is fun! Read Luke 2:1-20 and Matthew 2:1-12 from a children's version of the Bible. Then ask your child which character he or she would like to portray. Act out the story using whatever props are handy (doll, basket for the manger, towel or blanket for swaddling clothes, etc.).

For to us a child is born, to us a son is given. Isaiah 9:6